R.P. FLOWER MEMORIAL LIBRARY
WATERTOWN, N.Y. 13601-3388

ANN CLARK
NO WITNESS
NEW AND SELECTED POEMS

JANE'S BOY PRESS

Watertown, NY
www.janesboypress.com

No Witness
Copyright © 2015 by Ann Clark

Front cover photo courtesy of Ann Clark, Copyright © 2015
Back cover photo, author photo, and jacket design by Carlton Fisher, Copyright © 2015
Used with permission.

All rights reserved. No part of this book may be reproduced or republished without written consent from the publisher, except by reviewers who may quote brief excerpts in connection with a review in a newspaper, magazine, or electronic publication; nor may any of this book be reproduced, stored in a retrieval system, or transmitted in any form, or by any means be recorded without written consent of the publisher.

Jane's Boy Press
219 Arlington Street
Watertown, NY 13601

www.janesboypress.com

First Jane's Boy Press Edition, May 2015

*For Maria,
of course.*

TABLE OF CONTENTS

That Kind — 11

BOOK ONE: AMERICAN GOTHIC

American Gothic — 15

Hero — 16

Lake Effect — 17

Obliquity — 19

Woobie — 20

Definitions — 21

Unlucky — 22

TV Land — 24

Winter Heat — 25

The Wheels of the Car — 28

Shop Class — 29

Lewis County BIO 101 — 30

Banana — 32

Note From my 15 Year Old Self — 33

Skin in the Game — 34

Pareidolia — 36

The Bad Man	38
Back to School	39
Zebra Boots	40
At a Pizza Hut in Texas	47
Where You Name Them	43
Diving in the Whiteout	45
This Small Act of Faith	46
Behind the Door	47
Psych	49
The One that Got Away	52
Vacation Bible School	54
The Kindest Thing	55
Rapid Oxidation	56
A Fine Crop	57

BOOK TWO: NO WITNESS

Compost	61
Unmarked	62
Incidental Music	63
No Answer	64

Hot Stuff	65
Map	67
On the First Anniversary of Your Death	68
My Neighbor's Wife	69
Coats	70
History Lesson	71
Baggage	73
Saying It	75
Family Room	77
Runner	79
Oops-baby	81
If Wishes Were Horses	82
Invisible Woman	83
The Hive	85
No Witness	86
Acknowledgments	89

THAT KIND

I always wanted to be the kind of boy
who wore weathered black t-shirts
with a pack of Marlboros rolled up in the sleeve
high on the bicep, and Levis 501's
with biker boots because, obviously,
I'd own a Harley.
My hair would be black and just long enough
to be interesting, and I'd wear Raybans
on overcast days.

I always wanted to be the kind of boy
who took auto repair classes
while the rest of us were studying
Shakespeare in AP English.
I wanted to hang with the other stoners
and make jokes about the jocks, the nerds,
all the assholes and complete 'tards
who just didn't get it, and then
go down by the railroad tracks and drink
Black Velvet and laugh about whoever was
the most recent victim of Angie Daskiewiecz
who always had crabs or the clap or both
and scream Frank Zappa's "why does it hurt
when I Pee?" at the poor, dumb son-of-a-bitch
who should have known better but Angie was the only
girl in our small 70's town who would put out
and didn't look like the ass-end of a cow.

I wanted to be the kind of boy
my parents wanted me to stay far way from,
the boys with no futures, no prospects,
no goals, no hope, no self-respect,
the kind that always looked just a little bit dirty,
smelled of engine oil, gasoline, burning leaves.
I wanted to be the kind of boy
I wanted to fuck.

Book One
American
Gothic

American Gothic

The pickets of fences look like incisors,
teeth mouthing perfect lawns, and the lace
curtains have just been drawn back
by a hand we almost saw.
There's always a beheaded Barbie
on the sidewalk as a warning
and a Big Wheel jack-knifed in the driveway
where incoherent scrawls of chalk
are worn by summer rain that must
have fallen weeks ago. Even the tiger
lilies are dying of heat, and from a dusty
playground where the teeter-totter
scrapes across a rusted fulcrum
children's voices sing of Lizzie and her ax.

Hero

The woman pushing the shopping cart
behind Eckert's Liquor Store is really a super-hero.
You think she's a bag lady,
wrenching the wheels of the cart
through the muddy puddles in the black asphalt,
snatches of frizzed salt and pepper hair
escaping from a brown toque.

You see her every day
as she collects cans and bottles
from the ditches, makes a circuit
up Coffeen Street hill, through the plaza,
down Arsenal and over to the redemption center,
her mottled Australian Shepherd wrapped
in a baby quilt and wearing a bomber hat.

He's her sidekick, and the cans are landmines
or the components for a laser beam
she'll assemble down on Pearl Street,
where the world is saved every day
to the tune of just under ten dollars,
enough to buy a trip to the moon
on Night Train or Thunderbird.

LAKE EFFECT

On Thursday, another two feet of snow
falls in twelve hours of lake effect,
and the Jefferson County Sheriff arrests
Misty Kramer for discharging a firearm
within 600 feet of an occupied residence.

It has been snowing since November,
the banks so high, cars creep
into intersections, as if neighbors
peeping around a hedge;
and the banks cannot be cut down
or back, filled with fallen branches
from an ice storm, and mined
with yards of electrical cable
crews flung aside on ever-narrowing roads.

It has been snowing forever;
it feels like forever tending bar
at the Duck Inn when a husband
has been on disability seven years,
doesn't work, but never seems
to miss bass fishing or deer hunting.
"But he can't lift his wide ass
off the couch to wash a dish
or do a load of laundry,"
Misty tells the regulars.
When she comes home after a double
and he is parked right where she left him,
watching the Winter Olympics from Sochi,
she shoots the TV twice with a 30.06
and then drops it into the bay
because what blooms beneath the snow
is rage and dysfunction, icy cold,
and backed up with fire power.

Asked by the local paper for comment,
Misty says, "Do you need more time

to study the menu, or can I take your order?
The meatloaf platter is good, and
we swear by our fries."

Obliquity

She irons shirts with just
a hiss of Niagara starch,
the cotton still fresh from the line,

grinds coffee beans, waiting for
whistle of steam from the kettle,
pours water over grounds
in a French press,

arranges ragged wildflowers,
whose shabby disorder fills
a blue mason jar
on the window ledge
by the bed,

spreads linens, high like
parachute silk, smooths the cool sheets,
plumps pillows, and lets a fan slowly
swing its head, humming in twilight.

Women of her kind
have been taught to speak love
in these oblique terms.

Woobie

So it wasn't the first time they'd slept together,
but it was the first time they'd *slept* slept together,
and she was awakened by this really weird sucking sound.

It was a wet sound,
not just a sucking, but a slurping sound,
and she knew he didn't have any animals—
no dog or cat—so as she went
from just barely conscious to absolutely awake,
every terrifying scene from all the horror movies
she'd ever watched replayed in her head,
vampires draining innocent victims
like greedy toddlers with juice boxes,
aliens scooping out people's eyes,
zombies tonguing brains, and she shrieked
and nearly knocked over the bedside lamp
as she flipped the switch, only to see her lover
with a small, bedraggled square
of baby blue blanket, hanging from his lips.

There are people who do this,
keep a bit of their childhood blankie,
rub the silky edging between their fingers
as they drift off to sleep,
nuzzle and even suckle it,
letting the old familiar motion
carry them back to the memory
of a time before memory when there was
nothing but warmth and food and safety,
the kind of safety some people feel
in the arms of the person
they are in bed with.

Definitions

We were 20-yards-from-the-filling-station poor,
100-feet-from-the-tracks poor,
in the days when the rail still divided the town by race,
Palmetto-bug poor,
where you learned to call the huge roaches
that scurried under the cast-iron bathtub Palmetto bugs
because it sounded nicer,
and you waited a moment after flicking the light switch
before entering a room because these roaches could fly
and you dreaded getting their hard-shelled bodies,
their wiry claws, caught in your hair.

We were pancakes-for-supper poor,
so that at least once a week,
breakfast would turn up again as dinner,
toothache-in-winter poor
because there were choices
to be made between paying
for a dentist or fuel oil,
and tinnitus poor from chronic ear infections
that prayer didn't cure, and the ringing mixes
with gospel tunes you still can't forget.

A cousin says she didn't realize we were poor,
that she had a happy childhood,
asks why I'm so angry,
but I'm only angry when I drink coffee.

We were black-coffee, no sugar, poor.
It was cheap, and hot, and killed hunger,
the pot was on the stove day and night,
and there were only two kinds—
Maxwell house and Taster's Choice.

I'm only angry when I drink coffee,
and I drink coffee all the time.

Unlucky

I'm not sure what to call it,
but some of it's genetic since
Sissy's first was Siamese twins
joined at the head, and Rita's
last had no skull at all. Of course,
they died.

Sharon's girls looked
like elves when they were young,
just a couple cross-wired chromosomes
and near-retardation, and we've had our share
of blue babies, oxygen starved,
the cords wrapped round their tiny
necks as if they couldn't bear
the thought of life and decided
to get it over before it even started.

We are a depressed tribe, often struck
by dark moods and prone to fits
of anger and alcohol, self-medicating
with cigarettes and caffeine and
wrapping our cars around trees
and our legs around anything vaguely
human. Death runs into the road
to meet us or swoops down suddenly
as we shiver on the paper covers
of examining tables.

We aspirate vomit, breathe carbon
monoxide from poorly ventilated
heaters, fall asleep in the snow.

My grandmother was typical.
Baking pies, she had a stroke
and fell into her own oven, a huge
wood-fired monstrosity. My Aunt Kit
found her hours later.

Other folks have better luck.

TV Land

The TV news said hard times were
coming, which surprised us,
since we didn't know they'd ever left,
but someone said we had it good,
everybody with a television, refrigerator,
running water, not like grandma's day.
She dropped her first child,
was out of school at fifteen,
had false teeth by forty--
not so different for most
girls in the family now,
dentistry and college, something
they see happening to rich girls
somewhere else in a world
TV tells them has made everyone equal.

Winter Heat

We have been harvesting the dead--
a maple that
after some seventy years
has succumbed to summer lightning strike,
a stand of cherry,
dead from disease so recently
the moisture still bubbles,
gumming the chains on the saws.

We only take the dead.
The engines mumble and gargle
with the older ones
as the saws walk through the wood,
throwing sweet-smelling chips.
The trees have been downed, skidded out,
chopped into manageable pieces,
and loaded into the old wagon.

Maybe you have driven through the country,
after a "Bed and Breakfast" weekend
on the St. Lawrence to "view the foliage."
Maybe you've smelled the curious and spicy scent
of wood smoke carried miles in the frost.
You've sighed and smiled

or you scowled,
demanded,
"Can you imagine? Someone burning these beautiful trees?"
Understand.
We take only the dead.

The old people repeat the same old saw.
Wood warms you four times.

When you cut it—
there's more than just chain-sawing a tree down;
you have to know the arcane geometry of the landscape

and how to skid one dead trunk to clear ground.
Then there is splitting wood,
which, even with noisy machinery, is a matter of carrying
heavy chunks to the splitter,
placing the wood so the wedge comes with the grain,
depressing the lever, halve and halve again,
quarter, and toss to the pile.
There is a messy beauty in the blown architecture
as a tree is disassembled.

Wood warms when you stack it in cords.
You key and puzzle it together,
jigsawing it like the old rock walls
that stride unevenly across pastures:
carry, fit, balance, carry again.
Even on a cool autumn day,
the blue sky, pale and unwinking
with depths like a child's marble,
you strip off jacket, then top,
and are left with dripping t-shirt
while your eyes sting with sweat.

At last wood warms you
when it burns dry and hot
like valentines
half a century old,
flame caressing the cherry, maple, and oak
until coals glare orange as Jack o' lanterns.

We have been harvesting the dead
until my arms ache with it
and the small of my back stiffens from bending
and my legs cramp.
My hands are rough as emery board,
dry and cracked,
and the pallets are full from floor to ceiling.

If during your foliage viewing weekend tour
you catch the faint whiff of wood smoke,

remember these were the dead,
their hearts rekindled a moment.
You may think you see the winter heat
in the red and orange of the leaves
before you drive to your city home.

The Wheels of the Car

My second cousin, Tiff, had to go
to college to learn how to be black.
Bi-racial in Lewis County means black,
no matter how many little square boxes
ticked off with a number two pencil.

Wendy, her blue-eyed, blonde mama
couldn't tell her about African-American,
and her daddy was in Florida.

Marissa, the youngest, didn't win
scholarships. Senior year, on the bus
to school, as the wheels ground over leaves
of flame, a boy called her the n-word,
Rissa, thin as a dancer, fragile as rice paper.

Her mother called the superintendent
to complain, and he said Riss should take
another bus so she wouldn't hear
the n-word again.

I told Wendy to sue;

but then the town would know
Rissa was why the school lost
so much money, the reason football,
was cancelled.

So she drove her youngest daughter ten miles
to school the rest of the year, eight months,
while the wheels of the car hummed,
nigger
nigger
nigger

Shop Class

In seventh grade health class,
they split us up, sent all the boys
to the gym, where I presume they
learned how to rotate tires,
change spark plugs, and jack up a car.

We girls watched a film called
Your Changing Bodies, in which we were informed
exactly how spectacularly our flesh would betray us
and what to expect when that happened.
We were told our ovaries looked like flowers.
What is it about the female reproductive system
and flowers and Georgia O'Keefe?
All this budding and blossoming aren't good for a growing girl.
After the film, each of us bought a razor,
some deodorant, a bra.
As far as we knew, we were as prepared
for Mother Nature as we needed to be.

Lewis County BIO 101

They were double-dating
as it is understood in Lewis County,
where there has been nothing much to do
since the roof of the bowling alley
in Lowville collapsed
after a heavy, wet snow in February.

Parked off Hell's Kitchen Road
on a fine spring evening,
one couple in front,
the other in back,
they studied Applied Biology
with the seriousness
only the very young
can bring to such ridiculous postures,
necessitated by stick shift,
bucket seats, CD jewel cases scratching one's ass.

Remembering the old saw
that "If you can't be good
be careful,"
they used a condom.

A condom.

For when the couple in the front seat
reached their heady climax—
or
at least when the boy did—
in Lewis County,
female satisfaction counting for little—
the couple in the back seat
borrowed the prophylactic,
carefully turning it inside out.

It was an interesting paternity case,
a lesson in Biology

and Sex Ed all at once
and reason enough to repair
the roof of the bowling alley.

Banana

He trips over the cat one evening,
wakes up, intubated, catheterized, and
with an IV drip in the ICU,
where the noise of the machines'
beeping and whooshing almost makes up
for the silence of the patients and the hush
of the visitors, who are allowed
in two at a time, only immediate family,
and then are pushed out, fanned away,
by nurses, who move with the insistence of
fog banks or oncoming cold fronts.

Because of the tube, he can't speak,
and by the time a nurse finally brings paper,
he's lapsed back into the coma,
but this time he doesn't come
back out.

"Sometimes it happens that way,"
the doctor tells his brother,
who has driven straight through
from Cincinnati. "We don't know why."
And the brother wonders what his sibling
so desperately wanted to say before dying.

The brother takes the "personal effects,"
drives to the house to feed the cat,
hears an odd tapping,
and discovers a man
with a ball gag
chained to the bedroom ceiling,
feebly knocking the safety word
in Morse code

Banana, banana, banana....

Note from My 15 Year Old Self

That skinny red-haired freckled bitch
Barb Bradcock will beat me up again today
if she manages to catch me
in the locker room
and Mrs. Skinner will make us run laps
threatening to bring in the lunge whip
she trains her horses with
"to smarten you girls up"
I'm afraid to show her the note
I have from my family counselor
The one that says
I don't have to participate in gym
Lorainne Fesser, the fat girl,
tried to stay out of gym for her period
and Mrs. Skinner made her go to the nurse
and prove she was on the rag
which she wasn't
though when you think about it
that would have been embarrassing either way
and I'm not sure who
I'd be sent to in order to check whether I'm
having a nervous breakdown
but my math teacher announced to the whole class
that it's no wonder I'm flunking Geometry for the 3rd time
since my parents are getting a divorce
and my brother is in prison
so I'm not going to chance it
but Mrs. Tanner better remember
that I have another note that says
I don't have to shower in front of other people
she thinks it's because I'm weird
but really it's because Barb Bradcock
and Leslie Frye held me down and gave me titty twisters
to "make 'em grow" and it's too damned bad
my older self can't show up and tell me
what I'm learning today in school.

Skin in the Game

A political consultant is talking talking
talk
about Iraq again
as I'm driving home
from buying groceries for my bronze
anniversary dinner.
He claims we need to have
some skin
in the game,
which is just his way
of saying we have to show
we have something to lose,
that we are really putting
something on the line.
They use these phrases,
like boots on the ground,
without thinking of the people
walking in those boots.
Skin in the game, he says,
and I think of the tattoo parlors
that have sprung up around
Fort Drum, how we can tell
an infantryman by the harsh cutoff
of his tats at the wrist.
The tattoos mark the invisible
scars; that's what they're for—
to say the bearer can carry
this thing, a battle, a death,
another, until there is no
room left on the body
because all of their skin
has been in the game
too long, longer than I have
been married.
My one tat rides between my shoulder
blades, a lotus, not for eternal life,
but for the forgetfulness of the lotus-eaters;

forgetting the past is as good as a new
life, I think,
but the skin in the game
won't let these players forget,
as the needle buzzes, etching the bright reds
and blues into backs, arms, legs,
memorializing other skins, other boots.

Pareidolia

He can't walk through the detector
at the TSA checkpoint at Syracuse airport
because his prostheses are metal,
and he looks like some sci-fi Terminator
from the knees down. The board shorts
he wears don't screen others
from the hi-tech obscenity of his missing limbs
as security pats him over.
25, he's about 25,
and flying to Washington/Dulles,
as I am, for he waits at the same gate,
and idly pokes an iPhone.
One arm is ridged with melted
skin, candle wax, the kind that comes
from being on fire, and it's hard
to look away, not get caught staring,
but he is so familiar, there must be some
significance, some reason, and I wonder
if this was once my student,
this angry wreckage, who refuses to board
early with the old, sick, those needing
special assistance.
There must be some reason
his seat is all the way in the back
of the plane, just across from mine,
so that I must watch him again,
as he stows his ruck, knowing he won't
welcome any offered help, any thanks
for his sacrifice.

An older boyfriend served in Vietnam,
told me he got out because a sniper's bullet,
nearly spent, hit him straight between the eyes.
"I'd call that a sign, wouldn't you?" he asked.
Humans always look for patterns.
Another friend, who always carries a gun,
joined the secret service to avoid the draft,

but was sent into the Army to spy on our own
troops. In Vietnam, he kept track of how many
Viet Cong kills he made, how many of his own
men he lost. "It equaled out—16 on either side.
I maintained the balance," he said.
Humans find images in wood grain and marble,
see patterns in chaos, and the Virgin Mary
in an oil-stained driveway near Costco.
I see all of my students sitting across the aisle
on a plane from Syracuse to DC,
their legs stowed
in the overhead
luggage compartment.

The Bad Man

In the old movie Bugsy Malone,
pint-sized gangsters strut about proclaiming,
"we coulda been anything we wanted
to be," their suits so sharp, fedoras cocked
at angles, and as a barrel-house piano
plays ragtime, they sing how they're
"the very best at being bad" and wave
scaled-down Thompson submachine guns.

The humor of a puffed up, hissing kitten, extending
transparent claws as if lethal as a panther,
that's the thing in these bragging children with their
toy guns, all the talk of strength. Of course,
by mistake or with intent, they really will kill
one another, but these single, little deaths
seem inconsequential, not that we can compare
evil arithmetically, but if we could, this little
badness that so kitten-puffs them up, puts some
iron in their step, or imagined length in the cock,
this little evil doesn't measure up.

John cuts heads off men in the desert and dreams
the world watches, but the second time, the world
turns the channel, hating reruns, and by the fourth,
John's so small. Bugsy Malone's fake Tommy guns
are more compelling than such a very little knife.
We could have been anything that we wanted to be.
Oh, yes, we had that choice. And choosing to be
the very best at being anything--good or bad, well,
men go mad in that desert, mistake mirrors
for messiahs and swords for signs.

BACK TO SCHOOL

The books are stacked in order
by size and exactly aligned,
and he sits bolt upright, fingers
locked at the edge of the desk
like it's a car at the top
of the highest coaster of the theme park
just before it drops. His pale eyes don't
even flicker in a gaze that could be
looking at a mile of bandit country,
while the boy in the orange hoodie
slouches in front of him, and
a girl swings a sheet of sweet hair,
clicks her pen.

In the back row, a humvee is burning,
and the arms stretched across the desk
cradle a battle buddy,
a pack no one else can see,
a necessary gun.

Zebra Boots

Today she struts the hall in thigh-high leather
zebra pattern boots with 4 inch heels,
and she's just a-poppin' it,
with painted-on black jeans
and a scoop neck tee, topped by a
middie jacket, looped with silver chains.

Her processed hair is perfect,
long black waves that frame her face
and hang halfway to her elbows.
Who knows or cares if this is the work
of a hair press, chemicals, or
thousands of dollars of extensions?
Her eyelashes aren't any more real
than the iridescent mauve shadow on her lids,
but she is cutting a damn swath through the dulled
rural college students in this northern town
and not paying them any mind whatsoever,
and for just one day, wouldn't I like to have
ever had the confidence to swing a long stride
in those striped fuck-you zebra boots.

At a Pizza Hut in Texas

My cousin Charlotte was the family rip-Hell,
the one who skipped school to go smoke dope
and screw her boyfriend Chick Derose
in an abandoned house off Hell's Kitchen Road.
She was the first of my generation to have
a pregnancy scare,
and then another one,
after we'd moved to Texas and she defied everyone
by dating a Mexican boy—
and worse—one who wasn't saved.

Even after she married a would-be preacher,
she scandalized the church,
cussing and smoking cigarettes,
and telling her husband Alvin to kiss her ass
when he said she was a bad mom
because the baby got diaper rash once.

Big breasted and petite, Char
could only fit into stretch-top sun dresses
after that first baby came.
Alvin was spending all the money
on a mail-order preacher's course,
so she couldn't afford new clothes.

She was drinking sweet tea from a red glass
across from me in a window booth
at the Pizza Hut in Angleton
when the baby started fussing,
so Char pulled down the top of her dress,
yanked the graying cup of her old bra away,
and hauled out a breast so huge and swollen
she had to thread a nipple through her fingers
to keep from smothering her child.

She never missed a draw on her tea,
made not a move to cover herself,

though the paper napkins
would have hidden nothing.

In the mid-eighties,
public breast-feeding wasn't
a beautiful expression
of love and maternal bonding—
not in Texas.

I didn't know where to look,
so my eyes strayed to the table across from us
where two twelve year old boys
in baseball uniforms held slices of pizza
motionless, strands of mozzarella strung
to their mouths, eyes stuck to Char's breast.

The strings of cheese broke unnoticed,
but their pizza slices never moved,
while the boys' mouths still nursed.

Char had seven children by Alvin
and everything about her now is gray
as her old bra.
Her wild ways
turned to an aimless trudge
from kitchen to laundry
to a minimum wage job
at the Lowville Nice 'n Easy
while she waits for child support
that never arrives.

But I like to remember her,
free, and making it the best day ever
for two 12 year old boys
in a Pizza Hut in Texas.

Where You Name Them

I consider your children,
too many the family agrees,
shakes heads, clicks tongues.
"I don't know what she's thinking,"
Aunt Beth says, drying veiny hands
on housecoat as she turns from the dish pan.
"She can't feed that many
with that husband of hers,
he won't even look for a job.
I don't know what she's thinking of."
Her sigh is more a hiss,
air pushed under her upper plate,
as she heaps disapproval on you,
spoons sugar into black coffee.

I consider your children and wonder
about the naming of so many.
The first two must have been easy.
What woman escapes childhood
without names for those pink and blue
accessories of future-perfect existence?
But when your fifth was born,
how long had the name gestated?
Which was the first nameless expectation?
The seventh, whose birth was wrong,
and hovered between two worlds
in a glass box, wired like a marionette,
did her name come more easily than she?

Was your battered king-size, covered
with the stains of children and child-making,
the place where you named them?
Did their names vibrate in the stressed
springs, or did you stab a needle
in a page, trusting that blind thrust?

I consider you, your many children

and watch you shuffle in blank
circles from one room to another,
in the measured pace that marks
the time from one child to the next,
and ask, not what are you thinking,
but where are you when you are in
the place where you name them.

Driving in the Whiteout

At first you follow gloomy shades
of vehicles, like dumb beasts single-filing
through storms of an ice age,
just head-to-ass walking into whatever
chasm they'll find all the dead
mammoths frozen in when the glaciers
finally thaw millennia from now.
Then you realize the shadow in front
is gone, no slightest glimmer
of taillights, so you follow
tire tracks and hope they don't
lead to a ditch, but there aren't ditches,
and you keep on the tracks, pray
no one has suddenly stopped
or the tracks don't disappear.

I always thought I would know,
"At last, I am an adult," and
when I didn't, I imitated adults,
doing the expected, following patterns
laid by those who went before.
I wonder if they also
lost the horizon and the road,
were blinded in snow,
white-knuckling the wheel,
just trying to get home.

This Small Act of Faith

We never look when we swing our legs
over the side of the bed and stand.
We never look first to make sure
the floor is there.
Such is our faith that something solid
will hold us up, even when we vault
into the midnight,
wake in strange hotels,
or the borrowed top bunk
in some friend's children's room.

This small act of faith, as lovely
as it is foolish, must be human,
for my old dog checks each time
he jumps from our bed, carefully gauging
the distance to the floor, assessing
potential hazards and obstacles,
as if he believes his entire world
could have changed while he slept,
as if burglars might have come into the house
and rearranged furniture during the night,
or the architecture altered,
or the bed itself have flown
to some far-off precipice.

Behind the Door

At fifty, Grandmother became enraptured
with Spiegel catalogs, and while her husband
worked long hours at the Ethan Allen mill,
she would turn the bright, slick pages,
drink vodka and Sprite, and fill out orders.
She bought on credit, jewel-toned
blouses and palazzo pants, strappy sandals,
and chunky bracelets with matching earrings.

The best-dressed barfly at the legion hall,
she rode a stool from open to close,
peep-toe shoes showing red nails,
fingers studded with cocktail rings as she lit
cigarettes and tossed her red hair.
When Grandfather found the bills
she hid, she'd spent thousands on credit.

The aunts said Grandma had a stroke.
I remember the light in the long staircase
looked like a hanged man as we climbed
to her room, where she lay, jaw dropped,
ruby shirt vivid on the pale skin of her throat.
She couldn't speak, groaned—kept pointing
to the door, to her face, so urgently.

At the ER, the doctor told us it wasn't
a stroke; her jaw was dislocated.
"Probably a sudden blow,"
he said. "Did she fall?"

Grandfather burned the catalogs,
worked overtime, nearly lost the house.

The family never speaks of this.
Though Grandpa is dead,
even Grandmother says nothing,
as if her jaw were still hanging,

her eyes flickering toward a door
that might fly open any moment.

Psych

You'll think I'm lying
when I tell you that Peter,
who was raised by tenured
psychology professors from Yale,
only knew that he'd been bad
when he got home from school
and discovered that a favorite toy
was missing, given to the grad students
for their children to play with.

No mention would ever be made
of the particular fault.
His red tricycle with the bulb
horn would just be gone,
or his model of an Apollo
spaceship would have flown forever
out of his personal orbit.

Somehow, they always knew
which were his favorites
and where he had hidden them.

They even knew when he hid
a Stretch Armstrong he didn't care about
as a decoy
and only played with things he really liked
in the dark hours after midnight.

I imagine him,
a small brown haired boy
in flannel pajamas,
quietly running Hot Wheels down the
orange tracks that had to be disassembled
and put back into the box,
so carefully as to seem to have never been opened.
"Vrrooom," he whispers. "Vrrooom, vroom!"

Then, one day, after scoring less than
perfect on a spelling test,
or failing to put away clothing,
or not eating his beets or getting a bad report
from his cello teacher or not wiping his shoes
or slouching or any of a million possibilities,
he comes into his room in New Haven
and the box of tracks and all the little cars are gone,
having raced out of the house
and into some graduate student's apartment.

Peter bit his nails,
chewing, gnawing away at them,
and at first it must have been
a bloody business.

He'd been at it for years
when I met him,
and he had no nails at all,
his fingers wide as teaspoons,
topped with flat empty nailbeds.

No one wanted to ask about it
in case he'd been tortured
by South American drug lords,
his fingernails sent in a manila envelope
as "signs of life," but finally someone
raised the subject, and he shrugged,
"I'm a nail-biter."

He made no connection
between his fat, declawed fingers
and "Patrick" and "Susan,"
the ones who'd raised him,
and he kept his apartment
as Spartan as a monk's cell,
claiming, "I like to travel light,"
then inserting a soggy index finger
into the dark cave of his mouth

like a cigarette.

The One that Got Away

He's somewhere pinning his socks together
exactly as he used to before washing them.
He claimed that way he never lost one
and they were easier to mate
when he took them from the dryer.

I see him, chewing his lower lip
as he stabs a pair of athletic socks.
"They only cost five dollars
for six pair," I told him,
but he would insist on this tidy ritual
and then explain how organizing a spice rack
alphabetically was sensible.

He is somewhere in Ohio,
impaling socks and balding,
married these twenty years,
and tenured in Physics,
the first to love me and first
to engage in the awful ritual
of driving to the airport.

He had a birth defect--
I mean, beyond his dreadful tidiness.
His kneecaps were on the insides of his legs,
and he walked splay legged,
but what does that matter if he's brilliant,
a physicist—and—well, you can overlook
safety pinning socks.
But when he picked me up at the
Dallas-Fort Worth Airport, though I pretended
not to hear, a four year old boy pointed
at my bow-legged lover and shouted,
"Look Dad, a frog!"

We went back to school,
and a few weeks later I started a fight

about laundry, and now he is somewhere
in Ohio and knows where his socks are,
and I am married to a straight-legged man.

Vacation Bible School

My mother--the atheist—

exhausted by our experiments
with gravity and fire

sent my brother and me
to every summer vacation Bible school
in a thirty mile radius

We sang
until we were tired—
"Lift Jesus Higher"
and "Father Abraham"—
as we marched and waved our arms

I remember grape Kool-Aide
watery and tepid
and Rice Krispie Treats
melting in my hand
the marshmallow sticking
to pages of the lessons

In the late heat of afternoons
we returned and
mother
sent us out to play

never asked what we had learned

never saw me
in the dust of the drive

crying
that the earth would surely open
and Hell swallow our family whole

THE KINDEST THING

They look like they are wearing Dutch shoes
these ponies the neighbor has neglected.
Their hooves have grown out
six inches beyond the ends of their feet
and are curling up.
The horses hobble,
crippled and ungainly, shaggy creatures,
to whom the farmer sometimes remembers
to throw a bale or two of hay.

"Don't make trouble," your father says
when you claim this is cruelty,
but you watch the animals
creeping in the freezing rain,
and one day,
you do—
you make the call,
and your neighbor becomes your enemy
after the vet shoots
the two shivering ponies.

Rapid Oxidation

The world burns slowly.
Giant craters pock the Arctic,
first one, then three. Now scientists
say there are many more,
at least twenty blown through shelves
of thinning ice by methane, trapped
far below. It is imperative, they say,
that we investigate, find the cause,
but dangerous.

A thing is just always there.
The dog jumps easily onto
the bed or runs to fetch
his yellow ball. Your friend's voice
answers the phone when you call,
and the word for spoon twitches
on your lips without work. You say
spoon, puckering as for a kiss.

No one expected chasms breaking
through the ice, and no one saw it
happen, though it was violent and loud.
Far away, a cold village reported
the bright light, which was methane
exploding. It's not like aliens took massive
core samples of the ice. Our world
is cooking from within and rotting;
just now we see the signs, the way,
suddenly, the dog can't quite make it
to the bed or starts to limp, lies down
panting, takes no interest in the ball,
the phone rings on and on, and you
find yourself saying, you know that
thing you use for food that's not
a knife or fork and is like a shovel.

A Fine Crop

Every spring reveals heaved stone
from the deep cold of winter,
and the farmers must pick rocks.

Those quaint old fences carefully
jigsawed from thousands of pieces
of shale, flint, and good post-glacial
granite are the ghosts of children,
bending, picking, wearing hands raw.
No North Country girl from the farms
boasts dainty hands, for picking stone
is knuckle-smashing work.

A cleared field casts fewer
debris in spring, but still must
be cleared of casual rubble,
leavings of earth's tossing in frost,
and a new field is such an undertaking,
even with modern equipment,
piles grow to mountains, and
the idea of buying decorative stone
at Garden Centers becomes obscene.

The not-so-locals trot out the same
tired description of our hard land.
"A fine crop of rock," they grin.
And when the worn men and women
of our land die, we bury them
and mark the graves with stone.

Book Two
No Witness

COMPOST

Your mother's face is under the leaves
beneath the maple tree; the pile
you used to jump into, laughing,
spreading the raked colors
over the cold ground, now hides
the gray skin of her forehead,
the thin stubbled brown hair,
going white as threads of grass,
and the dried china look
of teeth in her open mouth.
You should go and see.

Unmarked

At dusk
she slipped out the back door,
careful not to let
the rusty hinges complain
or the screen door flap against the frame.

White Ked-sneakered feet
glowed in the twilight,
marking her path beyond the garden,
to the beginnings of pasturage and tall meadow
where she began to dig.

Never a very deep hole,
about a foot and a half,
with sod fitted haphazardly,
but carefully tamped down,
lest the dead should rise.

In one hole, she laid to rest the sauce-pan
in which a red-eye gravy had been boiled to hard black crust.
Another night, she dug a shallow grave for a skillet,
ridged with bacon, seared into the iron.
A tea-kettle, boiled dry and melted through the bottom,
nested uneasily over stone,
its spout choked with clay.

When my father decided to expand the garden,
we discovered my mother's many victims,
whose voices only she could hear as the tiller blade
caught metal, screamed, and broke
while she locked herself in the bathroom
and smoked cigarette after cigarette,
as votives for the dead.

INCIDENTAL MUSIC

You will hate the music coincidentally playing
because what falls to the
floor
aren't your mother's intentions--
it's her blood--so much blood
your Aunt Ruth soaks a dish towel
with it as then
your mother herself
crashes to the tile,
clots erupting from her mouth.

Don't tell me you can feel it,
what your mother feels at this moment,
what Ruth feels each time she wakes
for twenty years, still seeing your mother deliver
a bloom like a placenta
in that final cough that sprays the wall
like a force from the center,
doesn't close her eyes
like a tired angel,
but stares at the unclosed circle
streaking white plaster.

No Answer

"It's Karen. Please pick up.
I guess you're not there...."
The message spindled through,
captured on an old-style cassette
answering machine, left one July day
hours before my mother bled to death
on the floor of her living room.

I would hear him playing it,
nights when he had drunk
too much brandy or Black Velvet.
"It's Karen. Please pick up.
I guess you're not there...."
the whir of the tape rewinding.
"It's Karen. Please pick up...
It's Karen, please...."

When Dad died, I carefully packed away
the answering machine, tape and all.

I cannot throw it away.

I cannot listen to it,
my mother, ceaselessly asking
someone to pick up, the ghost
of my father, winding the phone cord
around his fingers in grief.

Hot Stuff

She always said she'd been a virgin
their wedding night, pure as the white
lace dress in the wedding photos.
Not that my mother would announce
this out of nowhere or introduce it
into conversations on her own.
She never was one to click her tongue
at so-called premature births and then
declare her own spotless virtue. But,
of course, I asked her, though I can't
remember where I got the courage
or even my motive.

So many of the aunts, and then the cousins,
were so obviously, so visibly, so damned-
near-inflatably pregnant as they lumbered
down the aisles of churches of haphazard
denomination, the ring-bearer or flower girl
tucked up inside the bride, perhaps, and
the clergyman fretting over Scotchgard's ability
to withstand the ravages of amniotic fluid--
you could tell from the way he gabbled
the ceremony like an auctioneer,
the more swollen the blushing
bride, the faster the man would speak,
all the while probably wishing the church
had installed a Vegas-style drive-thru.

The expanse of taffeta, the number
of high-waisted gowns, my Aunt Ruth's
frowns all meant something, though I
only began to guess when I was twelve
and finally asked, "Mom, were you
a virgin when you married Dad?"
"Of course I was." She never missed
a beat, and the answer never
varied throughout her life, not even

after I discovered the truth about Uncle
Harry, and how Aunt Alice knew, and
the whole town knew what he'd done
to Mom when she was twelve and
kept doing for years

After Mom died, I asked Dad,
"How long did you and Mom wait
before having sex?" "Wait?" he smiled.
"She was hot stuff, your mother, a
pistol. We had sex the night we met."

She lied, though. She always lied.
It's such a relief, knowing we have
at least two things in common.

Map

Look for answers on birth certificates
and in family Bibles, the old journals
with spidery copperplate handwriting,
and photo albums with scalloped-edge
black and white pictures.
Go to cemeteries and trace shallow
carvings in worn stones. Read county
and town histories, news stories trapped
on reels of humming microfilm, and
look in the attic behind the rafters.
Pull up flooring, and take it all
the way down under the tile, past
linoleum and beneath the oil cloth
and layers of ancient newspaper.
Written on the floor itself or
on a wall stripped of lathe and
plaster, you'll find truth, but
not what you thought you were
looking for, not the thing that explains
everything, the unkind words, the failure
of love, the crazy, the beating, tears.
It won't explain them, whoever you think and
thought they were.
It can't explain you.

On the First Anniversary of Your Death

You'll be relieved the old dog didn't
grieve himself to death, but looked
perhaps a little more foolish and lost
than usual and took to chasing rabbits,
until hit by a snowplow in November.

Only the youngest of the grandkids
still asks if you're coming back,
and only when we catch her
playing with your jewelry box.
She's drawn to glittery things.

Your loving husband took your best friend
to the Elks Club Dance, and everyone said
it was good to see them both smiling after
such a long, hard time and that they deserved
some happiness, the knowledge of which,
should keep you warm beneath the snow 'til spring.

My Neighbor's Wife

Has a pretty skull, stubbled
with new hair and marred
by the groove of surgery,
just now healing over.

She passes her hand across,
wondering at the bristles
again and again, bothered
by the itching of growing skin.

"Leave it," my neighbor says.
"All right," she agrees, nodding,
"but when they leave, you're going
to help me pick these scabs off."

As we walk home, my husband
tells me, "She still isn't right," but
our neighbors have been married
thirty years, and we, not even three.

COATS

We keep buying coats
though there is no room
on the five foot long rack,
stuffed with long wool coats
and puffers, foul weather gear,
slickers, trench coats, goose down
vests, stadium jackets, and barn coats.

We buy them at thrift stores, garage
sales, the Salvation Army, on eBay,
and at clearance sales, refuse to part
with them even when the pockets go,
the buttons tear away, and the lining rips.

My father was the same.

Born poor and raised cold,
he had the thinnest, meanest coat
as a child and was cold always.
When he died, he had over thirty coats,
and I have them all still, so cold
from my birth, freezing still.

History Lesson

The new grass just rising,
trees only in bud, my father looked for signs
of old dumps heaved up by the toils of winter.
He wore his soot-stained work clothes and safety-capped boots,
and walked fields surrounding abandoned towns,
spotting pieces of red iron or tin, a glitter of glass,
the chalky grit of broken pottery, and then
dug with a short hook, scraped an inch or two
to see how deep the debris went, then further down,
examining unearthed objects to determine their history.

He collected antique bottles, hand-blown medicines
and inkwells, Saratoga mineral waters in olive greens
and peacock blues, and fruit jars, all the different sizes,
so old the glass ran unevenly and the tops attached
with iron vises and screws.

Bubbles were trapped in the thick glass,
and I would stare at them, waiting for them
to rise to the surface and pop, hoping to catch
them making their way through eternity.

Once, he rubbed thick clay from a small
knobbly bottle pulled from under a tree stump.
He rinsed it with water from his thermos,
telling me, "People wanted to be sure
they didn't grab the wrong one in the dark."
The bottle was black, coffin-shaped,
and embossed over with thick glass blobs.
"That's poison," my father said. He liked to know
exactly what things were, liked certainty.

He died on a Friday,
was talking to me a moment before
about going to The Bottle Shop,
where he bought, now that he no longer could dig.
There had been pain in his chest for five years,

His pockets were filled with Tums.

I heard the crash in the bathroom.

After breaking down the door and calling 911,
I tucked his penis into his pants,
before beginning CPR.
It seemed important at the time.

The Coroner's report said he had vomit
in his lungs, and I can't recall
if I cleared his airway—
his false teeth were on the sink—
but the paramedics could have placed them there.

I can't remember.
I can't be certain.
I'd like to know exactly how things were.

BAGGAGE

My brother has a cerebral episode,
what a stroke is called when
the patient has no insurance.
His vision's failing and his kidneys;
an earnest nephrologist explains
the stage four kidney disease
afflicting the 52 year old patient.
"My brother," I repeat; the doctor
has called Paul my father again,
and after years of addiction, Paul
seems far older than our father,
strong until death at 70.

Paul idly plucks at the thin blanket
with one hand, veins bruised by IV's,
slurs his thanks I've finally come.
"I'm all alone," he tells me.
"No one cares if I live or die."

He turns his face away, but then
craves touch, wants to be hugged,
his thin frame, a bag of dry sticks.

"Do you think Dad hated me
because I was a bastard?" he asks.

Every child plays that counting game.
He was born on Memorial Day
after my parents' mid-August wedding.
"I don't think Dad was my father," he insists,
his brain half-blown with blood.

I have a picture of my father at sixteen,
with his dog, a Spaniel named Baggage;
Paul is the spit from Dad's mouth.
I tell him so, tell him again and again
and remember our parents' baggage is always

nipping at our heels.

Saying It

When Uncle dies, I will go to his funeral
and snort when the preacher says he
was a child of God.

I'll roll my eyes when we're told
Uncle is in heaven, has been forgiven
all earthly sins, redeemed by the blood of Jesus.

When the family sings "I'll Fly Away,"
I'll wink at my cousins, the dead man's daughters,
especially Chelsea, whose stays in rehab and psych wards

made Uncle claim I've done everything I could
and who knows what makes a child go to the bad?
(maybe a little rape, I thought, but never said).

When they ask if anyone has anything to share
about our brother in Christ, I'll race to the front
of the full-gospel, evangelical church and say

God has told me to testify that Uncle followed me around
the whole year I lived in his house, his penis dangling
from the leg of his ratty, cut-off shorts, like a gray snake,

that he molested any female child left in his care
and raped his own daughters on those hot Texas nights
when his wife went off to Tuesday prayer meetings.

I'll remind the family how long they've known
what Uncle was, prayed over him,
and tried to cast those demons out,

but never once called the police
or CPS because no one could say it,
these things that cannot be said

because saying would have demanded action
and we are all—every one of us—cowards.
If I say I'm sorry, it won't be for speaking ill

of the dead or causing a scene.
If I'm sorry, it will be because I waited
until his death to be brave enough to speak.

Family Room

Not so much sitting, as perched on the edge of the plastic chair,
I check my watch once more, glance at the television,
which is blaring repeated nonsense phrases,
then turn back to the door.
Two grubby children in the Family Room
at University Medical ICU are playing
some kind of tag, which involves hitting each other
in the head with a chunky black snow boot and yelling,
"Got you!" and

I am waiting for Aundrea because if I go
into my nephew's room, where he is sedated,
on a ventilator, wired to machines and fed with tubes,
I may run into his mother, and we think
she is drinking again, that she has picked this moment,
after a decade of sobriety, to not just fall,
but take a flying leap off the wagon
because her son stopped breathing, so she switched
from coffee to ginger brandy, and fired a couple rounds
from a handgun into her ceiling, so

I am waiting for Aundrea to tell me
Doug's mom has gone home for the day
or finally been thrown out by security after having
a screaming fit and accusing my nephew's wife
of stealing Doug away, depriving a mother of her
most prized possession, a son's love.
But until she's thrown out, I am waiting for Aundrea
because the last time Jenny was drinking, she hunted
me with my own deer rifle, got my seventy year old
father drunk, seduced him, and tried to make him
sign over his house, so

I'm staying in the Family Room because I was
an obstacle Jenny wanted to remove
with a 30.30 shell, and now she's drinking
and armed and might remember

I had her arrested, took my gun back,
raised her children, so

I am waiting for Aundrea, and I am in the Family Room
because we don't have a family,
just hostage situations.

Runner

You sweep and damp mop floors
each day, and I imagine you
short, gray-haired, in the yellow kitchen,
between sink and stove, or seated
at the Formica table along the wall,
where you drink that one cup of real coffee
and endless refills of decaf through the day.

Sometimes you hustle uncle's clothes
into the laundry, walking crabwise
on stiff knees and a tricky hip, crawl
up narrow stairs to the bedroom,
and come down each morning,
one step at a time on your rump,
clutching robe over vein-splotched legs.

Nothing mars the shine
of the wood floor; the stove gleams.
No dishes are left to soak.

Uncle still works as a handyman,
though his back pains him,
a fall while shoveling snow;
you asked him to retire, but when
did he ever listen to you?

The same day you brought your first baby
home, your found he'd cheated, but he cried;
it would never, he would never, not again.

One night you stood over your daughters'
beds, cupping a handful of pills,
saying goodbye, then decided to live
for your girls and Jesus.

They're grown now, and you're still
in the yellow kitchen,

talking on your phone;
when family call with problems,
or the church prayer chain,
your knees fill with splinters,
but the sound of the phone
makes you kneel on the so-clean
wood floor to pray,
as you're parying now.

You're praying now,
but your daughters say you're
eaten up with fear, paralyzed.

It's not too late.
Get up. Get up,
and run.

Oops-baby

My husband was either the long-hoped for boy
or a mistake, arriving eleven years
after his closest sister and eighteen
after his elder. The sister nearest in age,
Penny, claims he was wanted, the heir,
and spoiled, but my husband remembers
nothing of his childhood,
not the merest image, not a glimpse
of a Christmas morning or the smooth
silky edge of a favorite blanket.

Penny tells me she came to visit
after her marriage, and her brother was sitting
motionless in the hall, while his parents ate dinner.
When she went to speak to him, she noticed
a treble-hook buried in the flesh of his upper arm
and tapped him on the shoulder. He blinked.
He has no memory of this, that oops-baby.

If Wishes Were Horses

That chestnut is called "Thinner." She appeared
when I started sixth grade, and my Uncle Ray
said, "Holy crap, what a hogger!" and made
snorting noises after seeing me in shorts.

The dapple pony is named "Pretty" and has been
grazing pastures since a senior girl on my bus
slapped my face and called me homely. The pony's
shy and quick, hiding in the pines.

The Arab mare and her colt are faster still;
they are "Loved" and "Special."
Hooves pound the dry ground
of the home paddock, and long manes and tails
play out their length in wind and dust.
My mother sang a lullaby about waking
to find pretty horses, and my horses all
found me, one by one, failure
after failure, riding hard.

Invisible Woman

I am becoming invisible.

Automatic doors slide open
for others,
even for children
who run at them,
never questioning that
the glass will move out of their way;
how shocked they would be to splat,
to flatten against the glass,
to fly into it
and lie like
a stunned sparrow beneath so-clean windows.
The doors don't open for me.
I walk up, and
nothing happens.
I wave my hands.
When another person joins me,
the panes slip away.

Today a motion activated faucet
left me with soap-sticky hands.
As I wiped goo off with rough brown
public bathroom towels,
a girl came out of a stall,
waved her hands like a magician,
and water gushed obligingly out.
Inanimate objects no longer sense my existence.
The motion sensors don't register
my presence in rooms;
after 15 minutes,
the lights go out.

It started when I began to lose weight;
at least that's when I began to notice it
but I also married just
about the time I got down to size 6.

And then the riding lawnmower
began to turn itself off,
refusing to recognize anyone was
actually sitting in the seat.
We finally deactivated the sensor entirely.

It's getting worse.
my jeans are Jr. size 3
and I buy my shirts in the boys dept.
People don't seem to hear me.
Sometimes my husband doesn't blink
when I speak,
is unaware I'm in the room,
startles when he discovers me occupying a space
he wants for something else.

THE HIVE

One night while they were separated,
he was disturbed by a buzzing
in the background of the television laugh track
and looked up from their giant king-size bed
at the exposed ceiling rafters,
where along one beam hundreds of furred honey bees
writhed and hummed their soft complaints,
a swarm following a queen to establish a new hive.

He used the longest extension hose for the shop vac
and suctioned the entire vibrating colony
into the canister, as he trembled,
checking along the walls, the blank ceiling,
the tumbled, hot bed linens,
then finally carried the vacuum out to the barn,
as it thrummed against his arms,
its endless murmur of discontent.

No Witness

I am wondering where they go to do it.
These men who never cry in public
must have some secret place,
some workshop, back pasture, or den
where they finally let themselves crouch down,
curl in on themselves, hug their knees to their chests
as they did when they were boys of three or four.

It must feel like choking at first,
the gasping, ragged cries of real grief
that cannot be contained
but cannot be let out in front of anyone
and are saved up until the only witnesses
are hawks wheeling over an empty field
or hard worn drills and wrenches in a dim tool shed.

How hard is that to wait, to tell oneself,
not now, not here,
and then, when in that lonely spot,
is it like a reformed drinker
finally throwing back that raw swallow of whiskey
or an ex-smoker lighting up?

You see them at the gravesite,
blank-faced, their eyes stretched wide,
and only that awful motion of the jaw
gives them away.
Otherwise, they might be at a cattle auction,
sizing up the heifers or deciding whether
this year is the last they will bother
farming it at all.

When my father-in-law died,
my husband never cried,
not the whole time we spent at that dreadful bedside,
watching a strong man go weak.
"If he can't swallow, push the pills in

and give him some water,"
my mother-in-law said. "He'll choke 'em down."

It took him too long to go.

But my father would tear up at the slightest reminder
of my mother after she left him.
"Are you crying?" I'd ask,
afraid his sorrow would drown me.
And when she died,
he was astonished,
never quite believing there could be a world
without her in it.

My husband is confused by grief,
patting my shoulder as if brushing off dust.
But after his father's death,
he was off in the pastures,
back beyond the far fields
where no one but the hawks could witness.

Acknowledgments

The author gratefully acknowledges the first appearance of the following poems in these publications:

"Pareidolia" *Petrichor Review*, Issue 10, August 2014.
"Lewis County Bio 101" and "Note from My 15 Year Old Self" *Ragazine*, February 2011.
"Unlucky" *The Gambler*, October 1014.
"At a Pizza Hut in Texas," "Zebra Boots," and "Where You Name Them" *Adanna Literary Journal*, 2014.
"Compost" *Storm Cellar*, March 2015.
"No Witness" *Poetry Quarterly*, September 2013
"Banana" *The Good Men Project*, July 2014
"Winter Heat" *Blueline*, 2009
"TV Land" and "Skin in the Game" *The Transnational: A Literary Magazine*, 2015
"Hero," "Unmarked" *Black River Review*, 2013

Many thanks to my editor and publisher Carlton Fisher, who is brave, tireless, and fearless. I must also acknowledge my debt to fellow workshop participants at Binghamton University and retreats at Mendham, NJ, especially Tara Betts, Abby Murray, Nicole Santalucia, and faculty members Joe Weil Leslie Heywood, and Jaimie Wriston-Colbert.

My thanks also to my colleagues, particularly Stacy Pratt and Jessica Pierce, who put up with constant demands for instant poetry reviews. I'm grateful to Christie Grimes for encouragement and lessons about writers' discipline and to Brian Topping for his constant good cheer.

Thanks to Laura Boss for the example of eternal youth.

Thanks always to Maria Gillan for everything.

Finally, a note of gratitude to the Sewanee Summer Writers Program of 2014. Many of the poems in this volume were workshopped during that time. I cannot express my debt to the patient and kind Mary Jo Salter.

Jane's Boy Press

Thank you for buying this Jane's Boy book. The mission of Jane's Boy is to help new, emerging, and established poets reach new audiences. We believe that poetry is alive and well and essential to the day-to-day lives that we lead. We seek to publish diverse voices that bring that insistent vitality to the fore of their work. Please visit our website to learn more about our press, our mission, our authors, and our future projects. Better yet, consider letting your voice be a part of the movement, and submit something to our manuscript review process or for our print journal. Don't let yourself be one of those voices that goes unheard because the best of what you have to say is locked in old notebooks hidden in attic boxes or shoved inside a dresser drawer. Share what you have to say with us, and we may be able to help you share it with the world.

www.janesboypress.com

Made in the USA
Middletown, DE
24 May 2015